T0368532

To order additional copies of this book, contact:
Xlibris
844-714-8691
www.Xlibris.com
Orders@Xlibris.com

Book Designer: Michael E Anthony

ISBN: Softcover 978-1-4134-1311-3

Print information available on the last page

Rev. date: 01/19/2021

VISIONS AND STORIES OF A
CHILDHOOD IN THE **HOLOCAUST**

CECYLIA BITTER FEDERMAN
AND JERZY BITTER

ACKNOWLEDGEMENTS AND DEDICATION

This work was done thanks to the loving support and help of Marianne and Suzanna Walters of Washington D.C. Special thanks also go to two women in Florida: Hyla Levine of the National Council of Jewish Women, Boca-Delray Section, for the time and labor she gave to editing the work and to the love and care of Malka Osserman, my social worker at the Ruth Rales Jewish Family Service who gave me much needed emotional support. Encouraging words and recognition came from the U.S. Holocaust Museum in Washington, D.C. We would also like to thank the Puffin Foundation for financial support.   This book is dedicated to our dearest Eva and our great friends, Sybil and Sol Frankel.

Group In White

INTRODUCTION

This work was inspired by a letter from the United States Holocaust Memorial Museum announcing a projected 2003 exhibition devoted to the children of the Holocaust. The letter appealed to us survivors for memorabilia from this period. In my case the memorabilia was close to me and easily available—in the artwork of my son, Jerzy Bitter, and in my own memories, as documented in stories about my child's early years of life during the time of the Holocaust. Most of my stories were told long ago. In fact, some of my tales were published shortly after the war. This collection is what I can offer now: new or modified memories.

Clearly, the sequencing of these stories is organized around my experiences with my son, specifically his birth and early years, as part of life within the Warsaw Ghetto and beyond. Every story relates the early childhood experiences of my son. My stories have, no doubt, greatly influenced my son's images. The pictures have no explicit or fixed meaning. Their often one-word title asks the viewer to read them carefully and develop his/her own interpretation. The reading of the pictures is not easy. They are an appropriately complex view of life itself, conveying visions the artist himself remembers from years back, along with my own and those of many other storytellers. This may also explain the dramatic or even sad mood of some of Jerzy Bitter's images.

IMAGE INVENTORY

COVER   Mad Village

5   Group in White
11   Loneliness
13   The Red Raven
15   Cemetery
17   The Road
19   Death of a Gladiator
21   Woman in Blue
24   Amen
25   Finality
29   Passing Life
31   Mountain Flowers
33   Rose Gate
35   Children of Auschwitz
37   Gazing at the Deserted Sky
39   Terrified Saint
41   The Exile
43   A Child for Sale
45   The Beggars
49   No More Light
51   The Red Tower
53   The Blind Soul
55   Blue and White
57   Deserted
59   Children
61   Shelter
63   Locked
65   My Sweet, Sweet Mother
67   Wave of Silence
69   Tale
71   Escape

For additional information about the artist and the entire collection please contact
Jerry Bitter at 305 West 28th Street, Apt. 12B NY, NY 10001

YOUR RESPONSIBILITY

In the middle of 1940, my husband Marek and I lived in Lvov, now a Ukrainian city under the Russians. With us was my husband's family. They all ran from the German-occupied territories — Warsaw included — to the eastern part of Poland taken by the Russians. One day in the presence of all the family I proudly announced, "I am pregnant. We are going to have a child."

"Mazel tov, good luck," they said. There were tears of joy in the eyes of our beloved Mama. Now she was sure that the Bitter "dynasty" would not expire. Her four daughters had not delivered what her only son had. Everybody was happy except him, my husband. "Oh no, no children now," he said. "We must wait and see." "Don't you want a little girl with pink ribbons in her hair?" I asked. "He is a sworn old bachelor. Not before he reached thirty-six years of age did he want to get married," said his sister Guta. Mama added, "Until the war came, until we ran from the Germans in a loaded truck, your sisters clung to their husbands, and you felt alone and decided to get a wife. Now that you have a wife, pregnant already, you want to wait with a child. Why?"

"Wait, wait," answered my husband Marek. "You know that the war only started. It will continue. A great war between Germany and Russia is unavoidable. At times like this you do not want a new baby. Let's wait." "But I am pregnant, and I want this child," I said. "Okay, then, but remember it is your responsibility."

This is when I heard the word addressed to me for the first time. The second time was when Yurek was about fifteen months old and we were living in the Warsaw Ghetto. These were the days when the Germans, with the help of the Ukrainians and even the Jewish police, were grabbing people on the streets and from their homes and shelters, people young and old, healthy and sick, helpless people paralyzed by fear, screaming and shouting. They were delivered to the *Umschlagplatz* and pushed into awaiting trains. These trains took them to their tragic deaths.

Some people in the ghetto were relatively safe, protected because they worked in German workshops. They were not paid for this work. Their only compensation was a daily bowl of soup and, more importantly, an *Ausweiss*, a pass that stated they were working for Germans-a document of life. For the time being, my husband belonged to this group. But I did not, because I always had the baby with me, which gave me no chance to work and live. Once I dared to go out from the place where we slept, and very soon we were grabbed. I was forced to climb aboard a horse-driven wagon, joining a group of other frightened and trapped people. Only by a miracle did I manage to slip off the wagon when it started moving, holding the child in my arms.

From that day on, there was no more going out on the street. During the day we would sit in a cellar on dirty rugs and pillows infested with bugs, bugs as hungry as we were. Nights we would spend upstairs in abandoned apartments, where people used to live. Now our suffering grew because of darkness. There was no electricity and no gas. Cold water was still running slowly from the sink. One night I felt an overwhelming need to wash my body. Someone said that in the neighboring apartment "thin" gas was coming out. I went there, warmed some water in a pot and happily began to carry it to our place. But suddenly I fell into a little opening in the kitchen floor, leading to a cellar. It was invisible in the semidarkness. Hurt in several places and in deep shock, I went back to my people. Laying in bed I desperately considered what I needed to do. I touched the child with love and decided to act in order to save him and myself. No family ties now, just the two of us.

There was an alarming need to answer the question of how to save our life. What to do? I must take a chance even of being killed. I have to go out of the Ghetto. I look "good" (i.e. not Jewish, speak perfect Polish). Neither the looks nor the speech will betray me. I had the address of a woman who did not know me or want us, but I decided to take a chance knocking at her door. She would not betray us and might even help us. She had contacts with the partisans living in the forests where I would like to be. Later I learned that no children were allowed with the dangerous people fighting in the woods. I also had the names of my two Polish teachers. I did not have their addresses, but I hoped to find them and get help.

In the silence of the night I went to the place where my husband was. I told him of my crazy-sounding plan to sneak out of the ghetto and seek help among the few Polish people I knew. "I have to leave you all," I said. "What's the use of being together? We are not together anyway. Together we will be taken to death." Fruma [Fruma Miedzinski], his sister, had decided to remain with her beautiful five-year-old daughter, Elizabeth, and together they had been driven to their execution.

Fruma even had an *Ausweiss*, because she had been working for the Germans. But when the police needed more human beings to fill the quota of daily deliveries to the death camps, children were taken by force-in spite of the promise that a child would be left in security if the mother worked. So Fruma was the first of the family to be taken, along with her child Elizabeth, to death. Think: Fruma was twenty-eight or thirty, Elizabeth five years old. These were our thoughts, not words spoken. What my husband said was, "Whatever you will do is better than this, here, now. Go and save our son. I believe in you, and it is your sense of responsibility." Right, it was my responsibility.

The next day some contacts and a little money were found for us. With my only child in my arms and a small bag on my shoulder, I took a last look at the gathered family-no words, no crying, no emotions were shown. The old Mama could not understand where I was taking her only son's baby, the one who was meant to carry on the Bitter dynasty. She stretched out her arms towards me, but I was already on my way out — no hesitation, just determination.

Loneliness

CONTRIBUTION

It was early summer of 1941. We lived in Lvov, a big city with a mostly Ukrainian population. The Germans had already conquered the area, keeping the people in fear and uncertainty about the future. Yet, the Ukrainians lived with great hopes and expectations; they even hoped to get national independence that was promised by the Germans as a reward for collaboration.

Needless to say, they were deeply disappointed. In exchange for generous collaboration (in many shameful ways) the long-expected "free Ukraine" was given only in the form of a newspaper with this title. Another reward was the permission to chase out the Jews and take their apartments with all of their belongings. The Germans wished to speed up creation of the ghetto, first for this group of newly homeless people like us, then for all Jews in torn and nearby villages.

As terror was growing, Jews who did not have to leave their homes would not go. On the streets the Jews were beaten, humiliated, and ordered to do some useless and degrading work. All was done for the amusements of the Germans and Ukrainians. At that time, my child was only several months old. Seldom did we leave home, but one day my family asked me to go to the center of the city and sell the only piece of jewelry we had. Money was badly needed, because the Jews were ordered to pay a contribution to the war effort. It was an obligatory participation by the Jews in the German war. The item to be sold was a man's gold pocket watch with several engraved covers. It had belonged to my father, who gave it to us as a wedding present.

I knew the soldiers liked watches, because watches were precious, easy to hide and easy to send home to families. I saw one friendly-looking soldier. I approached him, but I was too frightened to say a word because my German sounded so much like Yiddish. "Do not be afraid of me. I am Austrian, not German. What do you want?" he asked. I simply said, "Would you buy from me this watch? I need money to pay a contribution to the authorities, for me, for my family, and even for this child. He is just a baby but already counted as a 'head' and obliged to pay." One could see the confusion on the man's face. Although it was strictly verboten, he was tempted and bought my father's watch. It was not expensive and very nice. I often wonder: Did he survive the war, this nice Austrian man? Did he ever wear my father's watch, enjoying the spoils of the war, those things taken by force?

The Red Raven

DILEMMA

I have to admit that I did not suffer during the war as badly as some survivors who toiled in concentration camps, who were beaten in prisons, and so on. They were so deeply hurt and confused that later many would not be able (or willing) to talk about the events. I did not experience any kind of horrors except a feeling of helplessness, hunger, humiliation, and constant fear of being discovered, a constant need to play a role of someone other than myself.

My child was more than my responsibility; he became my mascot. He was as important to me as I was to him. Together we would survive. I would have to make fast choices and decisions, all by myself. One event shows the dilemma that I faced and to which I can't find an answer, even now, almost sixty years later. I can only remain silent when my son says, "Still you left me alone."

I was in a large apartment in Warsaw where I was lucky to work as a maid. The work was hard, but I was allowed to have my child with me. He was a quiet child, even too quiet as a playmate to Janush, my employer's grandson. Janush was her only reason to live after her husband, daughter, and son-in-law, (Janush's parents), were taken away by the Gestapo. The three-year-old child did not understand the tragedy that happened in the family. He had a happy disposition, was very alert and lively. My son, whether because of a different nature or a different upbringing, had other needs and ways of behavior. I liked Janusz's joyful behavior, but I preferred Yurek's disposition. It was easy to have him around and do my work.

My child slept in one small bed in a little servant's room located between the dining room and the kitchen. The kitchen had its own exit and narrow stairs leading to the coal cellar and backyard. As usual in the afternoon, Yurek was sleeping. Suddenly from the front part of the apartment our tenant Wanda came rushing up. She was a Jewish woman hiding in the front room of the apartment. Wanda and I were both suspicious of each other being Jewish, but we kept to ourselves. She was living in secrecy, paying for the hiding. I had to go out daily and play the role of a Christian maid, a woman from a small distant town who had lost her husband and her home. Wanda, deadly frightened, said, "The Gestapo is in the apartment. Let's run downstairs and hide in the cellar."

Yes, but what about my child? In one moment I had to decide: Should I wake him, grab him, and run? He will certainly get frightened. He will scream, and the noise will betray us-the Gestapo was so close and alert. To leave him sleeping could save our lives. But if I were seized, how would he exist? And what if the Gestapo found him alone, hidden in a servant's room with me away in hiding? This was my dilemma in 1942, and it is still with me.

Cemetery

FOOD FOR THE BABY: IN THE WARSAW GHETTO

The baby was approaching his first birthday. His main food came from his mother's breast, but this was not satisfactory. I myself was starving so neither the quality nor the quantity of the milk was good enough. The paleness of his face, visibly rachitic foot, weakness, and apathy were apparent. A doctor examined the child and recommended a bowl of soup daily. But the soup had to be cooked with a veal bone. "A veal bone, doctor? Where would we get money to buy it? A barley soup, with a horse bone, we could get. Do you know how good this soup tastes? If we could only get the bone." Horses could be seen in the ghetto, lean, meager, pulling wagons with dead bodies collected in the morning from the streets, going to the cemetery. "Would this be good for the child also?" I asked anxiously. His answer was, "I said veal bone." And he left. In the end, the soup was enriched with the only available horse's bone.

Without the doctor's advice I knew well enough that milk was badly needed. But how do you get milk in the ghetto? If there were any smuggling into the ghetto, it would not be milk. Smugglers-young kids who would dare to reach the other side of the ghetto by crawling under or through the holes in the wall-would often be shot to death by the watching police. But others, lucky ones who managed to reach the other side, would run to the homes of friendly Poles. There they would be fed and receive some food for the hungry families back in the ghetto. The mature, experienced smugglers worked for the rich. Money, jewelry, and items of great value were sent out of the Ghetto to be exchanged for food, other necessities, and even sometimes luxuries.

But my question remained: Where do you get the milk and the money to pay for it? Well, both milk and money could be found. Milk was delivered by a real cow and there was one kept nearby in the attic of a six-story building (no elevator, to be sure). The money for milk in my case was supplied by our dear friend Rutka (Ruth Grynspan). She was a person who had grown up in the greatest poverty but who was always helping others. She had no children of her own, but she had a nephew whom she loved dearly. She developed similar feelings for my child. She was the one who paid for one glass of milk for Yurek every day. The way she earned the money was characteristic for that time. Rutka was working in a darkroom of a photography business in the ghetto. They were busy as people badly needed pictures for their *Ausweisses*, passes which stated that they were working for Germans. This document would protect the owner from deportation. So the photo business was busy providing Rutka with a good income. Our Rutka became a second Mama to my son, feeding him and singing at his crib Jewish songs.

This arrangement in the field of food and nutrition as compared with the desperate poverty and hunger that surrounded us was enviable, but it soon ended. The ghetto had to be liquidated. All people not working in German shops were quickly rounded up and sent by the thousands to the trains and to death. Rutka was among those sent to Auschwitz concentration camp.

While my husband was at work, I had to go into hiding with the child, of course. There was no food for us all day long. Only evening soup was brought from the workshops. It was only a portion of soup saved by the cook, an old friend of my husband.

This child of mine was extremely good, quiet all day long, as if he knew that one scream could betray our hiding place and lead to calamity. But he was calm. Only in the evening, at the table, when the soup was delivered, would he get excited. He wanted it all and would not let me eat too.

The Road

LVOV-WARSAW 1941/42

The little apartment I rented when I arrived in Lvov in 1939 became quite crowded after I got married and my husband's family came to live with us. This was when they fled from German-occupied Warsaw to the Soviet-ruled territories. In addition, in 1941, our son was born and soon, while hiding from the bombs in the shelter, he contracted whopping cough, which required special space and treatment. The treatment prescribed by a good doctor recommended baths: a few seconds in cold, then immerse in well-warmed water. The procedure had to be applied fast, several times every day, and in spite of the child's heartbreaking screaming. In addition, my mother-in-law would stand nearby saying, "She is killing the child!" Finally, we had to ask her to stay on the balcony with the door closed. Only when the bath was finished and the child was taken out for "fresh air" in good or bad weather would she come back inside, insulted and worried about her grandson.

These little worries were soon replaced by more serious ones. We were forced to leave the apartment and our possessions and go into the poorest Jewish quarter. The whole family was assigned to a single room and kitchen. This also happened to be during the coldest winter in many years. There was no heating other than by fire in tall stoves, where good dogwood and coal should have been used. But these goods were not easily available, unless one had a lot of money or could offer precious items in exchange. I had already sold my father's golden pocket watch to pay the "contribution," but we still had something to barter: We had three new bed sheets given to us as a wedding gift by a family friend. Peasants coming from villages would bring in wood on sleighs and exchange it for goods of that kind. That's how we got a load of precious fuel. For a short time we could enjoy the warmth; we could clean and wash the child, and wash and dry the cotton diapers.

In addition, we enjoyed the visits of Mina Sokal, my dearest friend from my hometown and my comrade from the Hashomer Hatzair youth organization. She was a nurse and had come to Lvov to work in a hospital. She managed to save for us some leftover food and to get us some cigarettes. Her visits were a joy for us, because she was always optimistic. But one day Mina just disappeared, and there was no way for us to find out what had happened to her. Our life was also very insecure, especially when one left the apartment. Once I was in the street and saw a truck guarded by soldiers with bayonets directed toward the people who were loaded on. The people desperately called to the passersby to help them get out — which was impossible — or at least to deliver notes informing their families what had happened to them.

Mostly we stayed home, except for my husband, who hoped to get some work as an electrician. One day he returned home and was behaving strangely. He was hiding his face, on which I discovered the red print of a hand with its fingers. Shame overwhelmed us and filled us with an urge to do something to change our situation. At that time — end of 1941 — news came from the Warsaw Ghetto saying that life there was kind of quiet, although the ghetto was overcrowded with the hundreds of thousands of people brought in from surrounding towns and villages. There was misery, poverty, and sickness. But my family, who had come from Warsaw, where their apartments had now been taken by others, hoped that their old friends would help us. So the decision to go illegally into the Warsaw Ghetto was made. The plan was that we go one by one, except I would take the child. Jews were forbidden to travel by train. We had hired a Christian man to take care of purchasing the tickets and to accompany each one of us. Every few days, the next person would be picked up by our man and carefully led to the train station.

When my time came, with the child in my arms I took a place in a wagon next to two SS men in black uniform. One of them liked children and took the child from me, put him on his knee, and gave him a lemon. He was eager to start a conversation. Not that, not with my Yiddish-sounding German, I thought. Suddenly I said loudly, "The child is wet and has to be changed." I took him and made myself busy looking for the way out. Our Christian friend, who could see my embarrassment, came to the rescue by starting an interesting conversation with the officers — in perfect German.

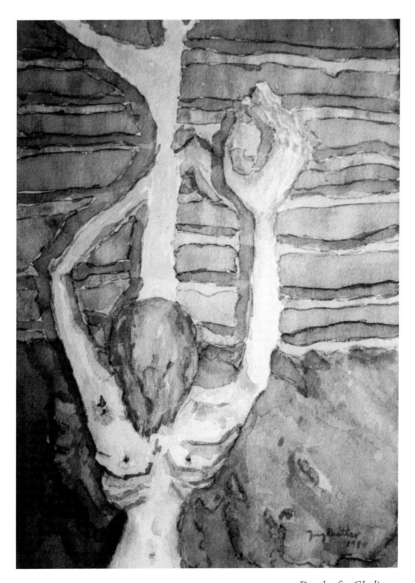

Death of a Gladiator

MY MOTHER

My mother was hardly a traveler, so it is hard to believe that she made the 100-km trip alone from Przemysl, a small town where I was born and brought up, to Lvov, a big town where my husband and I lived and where our child was born. She was highly motivated to come when she got the bad news that we, the parents of the boy, would not be having the circumcision ceremony to mark him as Jewish. She arrived unexpected and angry. She could not respond to our arguments that the war was unavoidably coming. "The child will be much better off and more secure if left as he is," we said. She was not satisfied with our promise that we would bring up a "good Jew." In desperation, she appealed to my husband's mother for help, but it was in vain. She refused any food or tea. Questioning our own Jewishness, she decided to leave. My mother left without even looking at or kissing my son, her tenth grandchild and the baby of her youngest daughter. Little could we know that a year later I would be seeking a way to even baptize the child.

Before she left she told me what the family had been hiding from me, that my beloved father died a few weeks ago. My son, therefore, was supposed to get his name. He was given my father's name, the name Fishel, but it was used only for a short time, while we were in the ghetto. Once we fled to the Aryan side, I had to change it to a Polish-sounding name, so I called him Jerzy, or by the nickname Yurek. My father's other legacies to my son were his brilliant mind, his earnest, friendly attitude, and his thirst for knowledge.

Mama was not alone back home. Hoping for more security, my learned sister, Sarah, a professor in mathematics and physics, along with her husband and two children came from a small town near the mountains to stay. They ran from the Germans but did not remain free for a long time. Two postcards were sent by Mama. One was sent to my sister, who had been living in America since 1927, asking for financial help. The second was sent to me, in the Warsaw Ghetto. Mama wrote, "I am swollen from hunger. Have pity and send some food." It is impossible to know how much of what was sent ever reached them.

According to the story of the house janitor, who was a Christian woman, one day Mama, with other Jewish people from the house, was forced into a covered truck. Choking on the exhaust they were driven to the woods. Already dead, they were buried in a common grave. As for my sister, she and her family had hidden in an underground shelter. Shortly before the liberation, they were betrayed, forced out and shot on the street in the bright daylight. It was my mother's youngest grandson, my son whom she had never held in her arms, who survived the Holocaust and went on to tell the world about this tragedy.

Woman in Blue

TO BAPTIZE THE CHILD

In 1943, I was working as a housemaid for a Polish family in Warsaw. I was not paid, but I was given a small room and permission to live there with my child, who was about two years old. There was not much food in the house, so I had to go to the nearby "kitchen" run by a charitable organization that provided the needy with soup.

Often, I would take along my son, although there was always the danger of being recognized as Jewish and given up to the Germans. This danger was especially great when the Germans would close part of a street, grab anybody present, force them into open trucks, and take them to the Gestapo. This happened once when we went to the soup kitchen. Luckily we were already upstairs and relatively secure.

In order to save one's life, it was important to have an *Ausweiss* or an ID document. I had one, although it was a cheap one that might be easily discovered as forgery, but for the child I had nothing. The only possible protection was to have the child baptized. He would get a real statement and also — it came to my mind — if I was taken there would be other good Christian people to care for him.

As soon as I met my two friends — teachers who took us in when we ran from the ghetto — I presented this problem and asked for help. Maria, the more religious one, wanted me to promise that if I did baptize the child, he would be brought up as a good Christian. At that moment, I remembered my mother, who had demanded a ceremony marking my son's Jewishness. My husband and I assured her that even without the ceremony he would be raised to be a good Jew. My embarrassment at the thought of breaking this promise was interrupted by the other good woman, Zofia, who promised to speak to a friendly priest about the matter of baptism. During our next visit, I learned that it was too late to register in the church book a child born two years ago. Christian children were recorded as soon as they were born, because during the war there was always a danger of sudden killing and death. In this case an unbaptized child would die as a …Jew. Little choice remained to me.

GRANDMOTHER PEARL

I have already spoken of Pearl, my son's paternal grandmother. She was the one who wanted a grandchild for her son, to carry on the Bitter name, and she fought for my right to have the child. She was also the one who had (silently, because nobody asked her opinion) witnessed my leaving the ghetto alone with the child. But long before that she was a beautiful girl in a family of several girls. I was lucky enough to meet another of those girls, Pearl's sister Nechama. In the 1930s, Nechama and her husband and children had left Poland to live in Russia. Here is not the place to tell Nechama's story, but it is worthwhile to mention that her younger son Feliks (now over 80 years old), his daughter, and his two grandchildren live in Moscow. My cousin Feliks visited me in New York in 1999.

Pearl's family, as well as that of Grandfather Bitter, had lived in a small town. How the marriage was arranged I do not know, but I do know that he used to say, "I had to go to the bottom of the sea to get this beautiful Pearl of mine." Pearl was a devoted wife and mother. Her sickly husband had to travel a lot. A trip to Warsaw, twenty kilometers away, took him a day and a night by horse-driven wagon, with stops at the inns to eat his meals. When he came home Pearl washed his feet and changed his stockings. She worked hard in addition to cooking and cleaning the house. She was the last to go to sleep and the first to get up in the morning. She was my husband's role model. This was the kind of wife he needed, he would say. (But instead he got me, a career woman with her own ideas and ways of living.) Pearl lost her husband when he was fifty-three. She was loved and protected by her children. Often she would listen to loud discussions regarding the views of the different political parties — Bundists, Zionists, Communists. These discussions were carried on by her daughter, son, sons-in-law, and friends. She understood little of all that political philosophy, but in important moments she would ask, "Is this good for Jews?" Just like these discussions she could not comprehend what was going on in the war and with life in the ghetto. "It is not good now, Mama, for the Jews. So we have to suffer and hide you. We have little food, no bread, no home," her children would tell her. "You can't see Fruma [her youngest daughter] and little Elizabeth [her granddaughter]." They had already been taken to their deaths. When my husband and the other people in the house were going to work she had to be hidden in the armoire and sit there for hours, alone and quiet.

When Pearl became sick and was diagnosed with pneumonia, the family decided: No doctors, no medications. Let us allow her to die. Better to die than live and wait for a fate that can't be good. And so my son's Grandma Pearl died in peace and dignity.

Amen

Finality

SHANAN

My husband Marek Bitter lived surrounded by his three sisters and their husbands. Each couple had a child. Guta, the oldest in the family, was really its head. Their father had died at a young age, and their mother needed constant help. Guta was a good person and had a wonderful sense of humor. She had the ability to dispel tension in the family, to put problems in proper perspective, reducing or bringing to zero their importance. Guta was a dressmaker, her husband drove streetcars. He was the only Jewish man employed in this field in Warsaw, if not in all of Poland. A jovial and very friendly man, he was well known and loved by his Polish and Yiddish colleagues, who loudly called him by his name, Hersh. Politically, Hersh belonged to the left — Poale Zion. Guta was still more to the Left, closer to the Communists. In practice, there were two distinct beliefs: first, that socialism was the only answer to poor people's problems and second, Jewish problems would be best solved in Palestine/Israel. While both agreed on the first principle, only Hersh believed in the second. Guta was sure that the social, economic, and even national problems of the Jews could be solved wherever they let the system change to socialism.

In spite of their differences in political views, Guta and Hersh immigrated to Palestine in about 1925. Their son Shanan was born there. Life was hard in Palestine. At that time, no comfort was given to the young newcomers. Hard work and the difficult climate became unbearable for Guta. She developed breathing problems, and they had to return to Poland.

Hersh found satisfaction in being admitted to a line of work that somehow was considered "Labor's Aristocracy." He felt free driving through the streets of Warsaw. Guta was a devoted wife and mother. Shanan grew into a handsome young man with a sweet face and almond-shaped eyes. He did very well in school, and, like his parents, became a good speaker and was Left-oriented when it came to political and social problems.

In June 1941, when the Germans were approaching Warsaw, the panic became overwhelming. Jews especially felt the need to run away. They were conscious of the great danger coming. The Russians packed quickly and rushed to the trains headed to the East, to their homeland. The men in our family debated what to do. Before they made their decision the train became unavailable. The only solution was to go by foot. Three of our men left, carrying only their backpacks. Shanan remained, persuaded by us, the women, not to go. We considered him at age sixteen, still a boy.

It took several days for our men to return, exhausted, with aching feet, and desperate. They fell into a trap, were surrounded by the faster-moving Germans, and hardly managed to find a way back. Shanan drifted away from the family. We did not see him, even later in the ghetto. Much later, we learned that this child had joined an underground organization for some military training and had become a fighter in the 1943 Warsaw Ghetto Uprising. His fate was terrible. While fighting on the streets of the ghetto or running from the attacking Germans, he was wounded. He was not able to run as others did. Determined not to be taken alive by the enemy, he asked his friends to shoot him. They did it. This is how the Holocaust took from the world a fine young man, our Shanan. He is memorialized by authors of books and by official documents on the ghetto uprising.

"GOLD IN MY MOUTH"

After a fast decision to run from the ghetto to seek refuge for myself and my child, I packed a few things in a handbag, took a quick look at my gathered family, and left without tears, kisses, or good-byes. I was accompanied by a Jewish policeman. He had already bribed one of the gendarmes who stood, one close to another, and watched the street that divided the ghetto from the Aryan side. On my way to this checkpoint I saw a group of Jewish women holding their children and being led by gendarmes in the opposite direction. Discreetly, my policeman let me know which gendarme I should approach. And then he disappeared.

I passed through the frightening wall of men in uniforms at the proper place. The bribed men let me pass the cordon which was a barricade of German soldiers. On the other (now Aryan) side I felt for a moment that I was free. Yet I soon realized that I was being followed by three people — two men and a woman. They began to attack me with words: "You run from the Ghetto, you are Jewish. You are going to Otwock [a suburb of Warsaw, where before the war many Jews tried to come to live or just spend summers]! We know that you are running with your child."

"Shame on you," I said. "Polish people should not let a Polish woman go where some business can be made." They answered, "We are not Polish, we are *Volksdeutschen*," meaning they were Germans just living in Poland, so they could do what they pleased.

While talking we reached the place where the streetcar stopped. I climbed aboard and saw them doing the same. While sitting down and shifting my child in my arms, I felt my armband. Frightened, I realized I had forgotten to take it off before leaving the ghetto. Slowly, I slipped it off and, leaning my arm over the window, let it go.

I had an address I was to go to and directions to the place. When I got off at a park, the three people followed me, and ordered me to go inside. They demanded my money. I gave them what I had but it was very little. They asked for my jewelry, but I had none. They searched my bag and found a piece of dark soap, the kind used before the war for washing floors or rugs. People in the ghetto were happy to have even this bad-smelling and unpleasant-looking soap to wash their bodies. Excited, they said, "Here you put your gold. That is how Jews smuggle their gold." But nothing on the cake of soap indicated that there was gold inside. Angry, they were ready to leave me and go when I asked them to leave me at least 20 zlotys out of the 720 they had taken from me. I told them I needed to buy some milk and bread for the child. Smiling, they said that all they would give me was some good advice: to hang myself on a dry branch of a tree. They said, "You *do* have gold, only we cannot get it now." They saw golden crowns on my teeth. And I was finally left alone, free to go.

What they said was true. I did have gold in my mouth. Soon, I had to ask a dentist to remove these golden crowns, because money was badly needed. But I was disappointed by the small amount of money I received for them. The crowns had been made when I was a low-paid teacher and spent as little on my teeth as possible; therefore, they were thin and weighed very little. I had rushed to the dentist, only to hear in answer to my request: "We are here to build people's health, not ruin it as you do insist." But the dentist did what I asked, leaving my eight teeth ruined and looking ugly. But this was a necessity.

The address where I was trying to reach and get help was of Mrs. Bierut, the wife of Bolesalw Bierut, later the first president of Poland. We knew him but never met her. She did not know who we were and how could we come to her home endangering her two children and herself. She wanted us out soon but let us stay to find a place first. I was trying to reach the woods and join the partisan fighters but they declared: no children! Mrs. Bierut's discomfort increased after a night of bombing the city by the Russians. We had to hide in a shelter and I had to face many tenants from this house asking openly who this woman with a child is. She is my guest, was the answer. Finally, she told me that was the responsibility for her children. I should look for another place. I had in mind my two teachers from Cracow now living in Warsaw but I did not have their address and several trips to Sadyba, a suburb of the city, did not give expected results. In desperation I decided to return to the ghetto.

But the day I tried to return I found the ghetto completely closed. It was a Sunday. No traffic was going in or out. One last time, I made the trip to Sadyba, where they were supposed to be. I asked a girl about the women — Maria and Zophia and she led me to their home. Both of them remembered me, greeted me warmly, admired my child, and in spite of the great danger, invited us to stay and rest. They promised to help me arrange our life.

After a few days I had to go out alone to find work and a place for us to live. My son, one and a half years old, was sick after life in the ghetto. He now suffered from dysentery. My good friend Zophia managed to find a family that agreed to take in my little boy for a short time. He was an addition to their three kids. They were poor, and what they did was out of compassion; I had no money to offer. For security reasons, they demanded I should not know where the child was. I had to accept this condition. It was the only, and possibly the best, solution. After a few weeks, a meeting was arranged. The child carried by Zophia looked pale and sad. Seeing me, he tightened his arms around her neck and would not go to me. This I also had to accept, hoping that soon I would have him back. In the meantime, he had to be with good people, and had to be cured.

At that time I had an alarming need for money to pay for the child's doctor and medicine. The money came from the gold in my mouth. Soon, the child was in better shape and I was able to take him back from the good people who had cared for him. Luckily, I had found work with a Polish family, and they had given me permission to have my son with me.

Passing Life

TO KEEP THE CHILD

For most Jewish people there was no way to protect their little children's lives-unless they found their way out of the ghetto. Some were extremely lucky to be helped by Christians. These rescuers knowingly opposed the oppressors' orders and risked their own and their families' lives. They did it in the name of their noble beliefs in human principles. These were the most charitable institutions — the organizations, families, and individuals who took in, protected, and saved Jewish children. Sometimes other motivations were at work, particularly when money was involved. Many people took money without even knowing how long they would have to care for a child or how much of an effort it would be.

In any case, a mother had to trust those willing to take in her child, even as her own fate remained unknown. At that time, I did not realize how hard it would be to keep my child and for us to survive together. When my friendly teachers declared that he could not remain in a temporary shelter, I saw only one solution: to "give" him to an orphanage, explaining my situation and asking for help. But that option was not available. There was not "giving" a child; the orphanage will not take a child when the mother is still around. A child would have to be left on the stairs of the home. Furthermore, these charitable institutions had very little money for food and the medical care of children. Mortality there was very high. Finally, the child could easily be adopted by anybody and disappear.

When I became desperate, my friends put me in contact with the RGO (Main Council of Help). They, in turn, led me to good people who could use my ability to work and agreed to my only request: to have my child with me. To rescue us, my teachers answered the employer's question on my origin by saying, "She comes from our College out in Cracow, where she was a student. No Jews were admitted." They did not find it necessary to mention that my admission was an exceptional case. Just as exceptional was my luck to be protected by such wonderful people and to be able to keep my child close to me.

Mountain Flowers

KOMOROWO

It was late summer of 1942. We were out of the ghetto and under the smart and loving care of my teachers, our careful protectors. By their discreet arrangements, my sick child was now in a place unknown to me, but under good care. I was staying in my teacher Maria's now-empty room and looking for work. In the meantime I had to handle another strange problem: The sudden separation from my child had caused a disturbing accumulation of milk in my breasts. At first, I was feeding the milk to the janitor's grandchild. The sick mother could not feed the baby, so I replaced her for a time. Then, I was visiting the nearby children's hospital daily. As payment, I received some soup or leftover pieces of bread and/or butter, etc. This good life did not last too long. One day Maria's friendly nurse "sister" [nun] took me aside and softly said, "People around ask 'who is this woman?' Please stop coming." I did, but did not despair because the RGO (Main Council of Help) sent me to work in Komorowo.

The place was located in a quiet, woody settlement with a convenient train running to the nearby city of Warsaw. I started work being a little puzzled by the family. She was a mature, though still young, woman who lived in the house with her seven-year-old son. The husband was left in the city. In his place she had a lover, a handsome looking man who was always wearing dark glasses. He would travel daily to work in a big factory. Otherwise, he stayed home. They both smoked cigarettes and enjoyed the sound made by extinguishing them in water. When I asked not to do this, they guessed that I used the butts to smoke the remaining tobacco.

They clearly loved each other. They read a lot, and had so much to discuss together. But there was also a lot of secrecy. All talking would stop when I came into the room. They liked my work. She said that she had always been convinced that a good maid like me should have a good education like mine. Once, in a state of satisfaction, she started a broad talk and approached personal matters. I interrupted her saying, "This we shall leave for our meeting after the war." But she protected her comfortable life jealously. When I was in need, I asked, "Would you permit me to have my little boy here, to share with him my bed and my food?" Without a moment's hesitation she said, "No."

Several years later I was on vacation at a prestigious summer resort, my son Yurek at my side. I was slim, good-looking, and well-dressed in clothing from America. One day on the boardwalk, a handsome man in dark eyeglasses stopped in front of me. I did not recognize him, but he knew me. He asked, "Is this Mrs. Cecylia? Is it possible? You are here, and you look so different." An attraction developed between the two of us, both Jews. When my former employer, now his wife arrived, she heard about me and about my being there. She decided she had to see me, "dead or alive" as they say. This time *my* answer was "no."

When I returned to my job in Warsaw, I found a bouquet of flowers and a package of cigarettes on my desk.

Rose Gate

A STRANGE OCCURRENCE

While I was working in Komorowo, I took a day off and went to Warsaw. My good teacher Zophia met me there and in her arms she brought my baby boy to let us see each other. Although I was more than glad that the child's health was improving under the good care of the two women — Zophia and the unknown caretaker — I was preoccupied with our immediate life problem. It was not only that after a few weeks of separation the child refused me. More importantly, I was asked to take back the child as soon as possible. The good woman had too much work to do with her own large family. In my mind, I carried the memory of the "no" answer I had received from my employer when I asked for permission to have my child with me.

With the visit finished, I went back to Komorowo. When I left the train it was dark already. My way home led through the forest of needle trees. Their aroma and beauty and tranquility around me made me feel vulnerable. What can I do all alone, just me and my child? Leaning on the trunk of a tree, I let my tears flow. My thoughts turned to my father. Long dead, he remained in my heart. He was loving, always careful in expressing his mind, tender and respectful towards women. He was the one who wanted me to be strong and independent. He once gave me one of his hand-made cigarettes which he made himself, saying, "If you need smoking for your independence, smoke. Here, have a cigarette." This was said when my mother would say, "Shame that a nice Jewish girl should smoke." Now my thoughts turned to him. Now I was ashamed of my weaknesses, but I also felt there would be a solution to my problems.

First I did not see anybody, but, I heard a man's voice: "What happened to you? Why are you crying? How can I help you?" asked the man, a watchman for this neighborhood. I told him of my trouble and of my need to find work with the permission to have my child with me. Like a father he led me to one of the homes and shortly, I was sitting at a large dining table, across from a woman who was ready to listen and help. "But first, before anything, are you not a Jew?" she asked. Slowly, I said, "You do not have to be Jewish-in these times-to suffer and be in need." She accepted this answer and quickly wrote for me two addresses of several Polish families in need of a maid. The first family lived nearby. The lady was impressed by my ability to do all the work in the house, even making preserves and sewing cloth. The couple did not have children. They like children, but no, no, they would rather that I give my child to some peasants in the country, paying for it with money they would pay me. This solution did not satisfy me.

The other address was in the center of Warsaw. I was informed that the apartment there was large and so was the family. I should expect hard work and no money. But there would be a tiny servant's room for me and my child. Yes, there was a little boy in the family and they would be glad to have another one — mine — for their child's company. The next day I got my boy, and we came to live there for the next two years.

Children of Auschwitz

KATHIE-POLISH HOTEL

Kathie was the only friend who came several times to visit me and my child. In the apartment where I worked as a maid and where my son and I lived for about two years of the war, nobody else visited me, nor did I know anybody else. Kathie came from a very poor Jewish family with six children, half boys and half girls; all the boys were communists. Among the girls was Mina, whom I've mentioned already as my friend from the Hashomer Hatzair youth group. This well-known family was under the steady watch of the police, and the boys were often arrested without reason, just as a "preventative" measure like before the First of May (International Workers' Day) and other days when demonstrations were expected. When all of them (or one of them) was arrested their mother could be seen daily, carrying a cooked meal to the prison located in the center of town. Some in the house had tuberculosis; others were in danger of getting it.

Kathie, the eldest daughter, was different from all others in the family. She was good-looking, well-groomed, elegantly dressed and was seen in the company of Polish officers. This was very unusual, and she came to be called "the officer's dame." While in my hometown, I seldom saw her, and I doubt if I ever spoke to her. During the time I lived out of the ghetto the general custom (or rule) for Jews with changed identities and were hiding among the Christians was to avoid anybody who looked familiar or who was somehow interested in you. The standard response was, "You have made a mistake. I am not the person you have in mind."

But when I met Kathie on a bright, sunny day on the streets of Warsaw, we both stopped. She said, "Whether one of us is Gestapo, I have to talk to you." She was still good-looking and elegant. She was warm and affectionate to me and my little boy as nobody else had been. She could see that we lived in poverty. She may have felt it dangerous to stay and talk with us. She quickly asked for my address and I gave it to her, although she did not give me hers. It was a risk, for which we could dearly pay. But she was so nice and friendly and was like a sign sent from my hometown, a promise of someone's closeness — something I had badly missed for a long time. "I am working in a German office," she said (she knew the German language), "with my girlfriend who is also Jewish." Anticipating the curiosity of my hostess, she said, "Tell your people at home that you met a cousin, and I will come to visit you soon."

She soon arrived bringing some goodies for the child and cloth for me. I cannot remember what cloth, but I do remember that for a long time I could not wear it because it was too good, too different from what I was normally seen in. I did not want to arouse suspicions, draw special attention, nor have any questions asked. Kathie gave me also an old blanket she used to iron on. From this blanket, I cut out and sewed by hand a little coat for my son.

Kathie managed well, working in an office and living with her woman friend. They lived, always watchful, and acted carefully. Her experience with the officers helped her now. She knew how to behave, talk, appreciate their gallantry, and tolerate their courtship. Kathie worried about us, and, unasked by me, tried to find some help for us. One day she came with information that a representative of the Jewish "Joint" (Joint Distribution Committee) organization in America was in Warsaw, in hiding. While in hiding he brought help to people, and I could also get help if I wished. My decisive answer was, "I do not want any help. Nobody should know about us and our address." This was my order, given without hesitation.

Not much later, Kathie came with another piece of news. She knew of an action arranged by the Germans themselves, called Polish Hotel. The action is meant for Jews who have relatives in America and have the means to pay for the trip and other expenses like a few days stay in Polish Hotel, transportation, etc. These people would be granted passage out of the country to America. "Don't you have a sister in America?" Kathie asked. "Yes, but I have no money," I said. She answered, "There are, among those willing to go, angels — people like angels. They are ready to pay for you and the child."

Kathie's enthusiasm frightened me. I said that it was clearly a trap. The Germans were using people's confidence in the power of money to catch the rich and to get them, along with their valuables, out of hiding. I appealed to Kathie to warn others against the action and against trusting in the Germans.

With the start of the Polish Warsaw Uprising in 1944 I lost contact with Kathie. Several years after the end of the war I unexpectedly met Jan, the youngest son in the family and the youngest brother of Mina and Kathie. He had run from the Germans early enough and escaping to Russia, he had fought with the Russians against the Germans. After the war, he settled in Lodz and was the director of a garment factory. He had no children, and with him ended the saga of a communist Jewish family. Jan told me that Kathie had been evacuated to a refugee camp near the city. The poor conditions in the camp and her susceptibility to tuberculosis soon caused her to develop this sickness. She died in the last stage of the war, one of its last victims. She was a dear friend to me and my child, a ray of sun in the dark days of the Holocaust.

Gazing at the Deserted Sky

MRS. MALEWSKI

For the first supper at my new job in Warsaw, I was to prepare fresh-cooked potatoes with milk. Nine or ten people were expected at the table: Mr. And Mrs. Malewski, the heads of the household; their son, also named Jerzy; his fiancée; my employer's daughter Maria, along with her husband and their son, Janush, who was my child's age; Grandmother Valeria; and my son and I. As ordered, I brought the potatoes from the cellar, where they were stored. I carried them in pails, two for balance, up five flights. The potatoes were small, and it took a long time to peel and clean them. I did my work seated on a low chair, away from the large table where the family was having a lively conversation.

Mr. Malewski was reminiscing about past good times, when they had held prestigious jobs, when money and food were plentiful. Often they would go to a bar for a drink and then out to beat Jews on the street. "Remember, son?" he asked. "Oh, yes, it was really fun," his son replied. Then with a little sorrow Mr. Malewski said, "Now we have too little money." Flaring up with national pride he added, "We could get money if we agreed to have a Jew here. But as long as I live I will not let a Jew cross my threshold." This was his declaration just when we arrived and shortly before the Gestapo arrested him, his daughter, and his son-in-law.

The reason for the arrests was probably their belonging to some Polish underground military organization. Indeed, with them gone, some secret knocking on the front door stopped as well, as did the regular visits of strangers. Now, with the three members of the family taken, Mrs. Malewski rented two rooms to supplement her income. One of the tenants was a Jewish woman named Wanda, who could not go out of the house for fear that her looks might betray her. Mrs. Malewski declared that having Wanda did not contradict her patriotic feelings. As for me, she had been assured by my teachers that I was not Jewish. "Maybe her husband was," they said. She was glad that Wanda and I kept our distance. Wanda belonged to a rich family that produced aspirin. Her sister, as well as her brother and his wife all were hiding in separate apartments.

Wanda's younger sister and her girlfriend once became panicked when they heard loud knocking at the front door of the home they had been living in. The Gestapo ordered them to open the door. The women silently brought the Gentile owner of the house and ran. When the Gestapo entered the front door the women climbed out of the kitchen window of their ground-floor apartment. Unfortunately, one of them broke the glass while jumping down. The Gestapo followed the noise and arrested them. The desperate family later learned that the Gestapo had not even really been looking for them. Their fear had betrayed them. There was no way to bribe the authorities for their freedom, as the family tried to do. They just disappeared.

Living with Mrs. M. was good for us. We worked together, prepared and sent out packages for the three in the family in concentration camps. We ate modest meals, took care of the two children, etc. We were always careful while talking. She was secretive and self-controlled. I knew how to keep relative closeness while maintaining the proper distance too. Not familiarity but respect was what she expected of me. She also demanded that her son show me this same respect. He would wonder why she wanted a married woman in her home, not just a maid he could order to clean and polish his shoes. He was not allowed to make such demands of me.

When the Polish Warsaw Uprising broke out in 1944, Mrs. Malewski and her grandson were taken out of town by friends. Her brother, a medical doctor, took me and my child to the nearby hospital, where we were given shelter and where I worked as a nurse. I did not see Mrs. M. for several years, not until my reunited family returned to Warsaw and settled on the less ruined east side of the city.

When we met again, she wondered at how my son had grown, becoming a good-looking, friendly, and outspoken boy far different from the one she knew. She still did not know that we were Jewish. When I told her, she asked why I didn't tell her that when we were together in her house. Did I not trust her? Moved, I answered, "It would be easier to tell you, but harder for you to live with the knowledge." Then I added, "I never doubted your nobility, but in those days nobody could predict what would happen or could foresee the results of the happenings. I was lucky to meet you. Thanks."

Terrified Saint

SECRETS

During the two years 1942 through 1944, after running from the Ghetto with my little son, I worked for a Polish family in Warsaw as a maid. The large apartment, with many people living in it, was full of secrets. The lady of the house was a woman of great Polish culture and a patriot. The family was impoverished now, but according to her husband's wish she would not take in tenants, and surely not a Jewish person, to increase their income. Only when the husband, along with their daughter and son-in-law were arrested, did she rent two rooms to people in trouble who were in need for a discreet place to live. That is how the Jewish woman Wanda and a Polish underground man named Marian came to live with us. All was kept in secret. Living with her family was Grandma Valeria, who was a mystery to me and reason for my fears. Tall and slim she would walk noiseless like a shadow in the house. She would suddenly appear and ask, "Where did you get this? It is mine," pointing at an old forgotten and abandoned skirt, almost a rag, given to me by her daughter that I had fixed to fit me. This and other unexpected memories came to her, the person who always claimed, "I do not remember anything. Don't ask me. I don't remember." But she did remember that the small piece of butter put in a tiny glass dish on the table at dinnertime was not supposed to be eaten by grown-ups. It was just for the children and used in small pieces with bread.

"The children did not get bread and butter today," said the lady of the house. "How could you—Cecylia—eat it all by yourself?" Frightened, I said, "It was not me, but Grandma Valeria. She remained longer at the table, and with a piece of bread consumed all the butter." I was afraid that living behind a wall of insanity she might betray us all.

After the tragic arrest of her family, Mrs. Malewska smartly ruled the house. We lived close but kept our distance. I wonder if she knew or suspected us, the tenant Marian and me, of a special relationship or closeness. Some evenings when all in the house were asleep, when the city and dark streets were empty of people and deadly silent, the two of us would meet and talk. He told me about his illegal activities in the Polish underground organization and his suspicions about me and my Jurek being Jewish. He provided me with a false identification document, which could help me if I was stopped in the streets by the police.

At that time, with my life relatively stabilized, I felt lonely and very much in need of a friend. There was not much room for intimacy. Marian had a roommate, an older man who talked very loud, and naturally this man was always home in the evening. They both like drinking vodka, and this older man even had a "delirious tremens" attack one evening that I witnessed. We waited in silence until it passed. His shame made it hard for me to keep them company after that.

One day Marian invited my son and me to visit his sister who lived in a distant part of the city. She was a nice and warm person, and lived alone in a comfortable apartment. When we parted she said, "If you ever want, or have to give away your child, I will take him." He had entrusted her with my secret I thought, but it was good to have a new friend and a place to hide my child in case of need. Would her wish to get a child be the reason for the invitation? This is my child — I must survive with him.

Time passed, events took us both, Marian and I, to different places. The war ended and I was again in Warsaw with my family. One day, unexpectedly, Marian appeared at my home. We exchanged a few words. Marian looked around and found me settled. "So you are here," he said, "and I thought you would be with me. Nothing for me here." He left and we never saw each other again. The story remained a secret, until now.

The Exile

A CHILD FOR SALE

It was a warm sunny day. We had gone to the nearby small grocery store to do some shopping. The owners, a middle-aged couple, knew us and spoke to us in a friendly manner. This time, the store was empty, and the owners were looking with great interest at my child, who was wandering about, barefoot, as he liked to be. He was two-and-a-half years old, quite pretty, and very friendly. Suddenly, the woman said, "It must be hard on you with the child. Would you give him to us?" And after a moment, "You will get some money." There it was again, an offer to give away my son, this time for money. That word: money, money, money, a desperate call I still hear in my head.

A Child for Sale

MOONLIGHT MARCH OF THE BEGGARS

The event in the grocery store when I was asked to sell my little son took my thoughts back to a scene where money was the loudest song, a call to a people in misery and desperation. It happened about a year ago, when we were still in the Warsaw Ghetto, before we left it to find our salvation. It was in the late hours of a frosty evening in the winter of 1942. Nobody was allowed on the street, just the police. The streets were empty; no sound came from outside. It was curfew, called the "Police Hour." Suddenly, those of us inside the homes were alarmed by a strange commotion. It was the noise of many people, walking, calling, screaming, and even singing. Frightened, I grabbed my child and ran to the window. A full moon lit the most unusual scene. Other faces in the windows around us showed the same bewilderment. Down on the street there was a parade, a march of the poorest of the poor, the homeless and the hungry. These people were not afraid to break the curfew. They were not afraid of any punishment by the police. They knew they were already condemned to death sooner than others by the harshness of their circumstances. Their misery had started earlier, when they were taken from their homes in the smaller towns and villages. Against their will, they were brought into the big, strange ghetto already impoverished, overcrowded, and plagued by typhoid fever and other sicknesses. As it was winter, the night was very cold, and the streets were covered with mounds of snow. The people wore only rags. Children were barefoot or had feet wrapped with rags or even just paper. Mothers were carrying little children. Younger people were supporting the older and weaker ones. Some were not walking but just jumping in order to keep on moving and fight off frostbite.

"Have pity, Jewish children," was heard the scream. "Money, money, money is the best thing," sang a young boy. "Throw down a piece of bread, a dry end-piece of bread," called someone else. "*Bony oj bony*. If you do not have the *bony*, it's a calamity (a *klug*) to you," sang another boy. "A potato, throw down a potato, even a rotten one," screamed a woman. "Hitler is cholera and takes away the bonys," continued the song. "Throw down a *groschen* [a penny]," begged someone. And "*Rachmunes* [pity] *rachmunes*," softer or louder they called, walking or stretching their arms to the viewers. Swiftly, the kids picked up from under their feet donations that had been wrapped in paper and thrown from the windows. Slowly, the parade moved forward and away. Silence once again took over the street and left us to contemplate the bottomless sadness in our hearts. A scene like that could never be forgotten by anyone present. The sadness of it remains in our hearts for as long as we live.

But an event like this led not only to desperation. In my case, it strengthened my wild determination to save my child's life and ignited an urge to distance myself from the crowd. I would not be one of them. I would find a way to be independent and solely responsible for the child. In the crowd, even with the family, we will perish, I predicted. Alone, there must be some chance to win the battle of life.

These feelings started in me after just two months of being in the ghetto. The time for action came a few months later, when conditions became worse and making a choice became a necessity. I decided never to become one of a crowd being led to an unknown destiny.

The Beggars

EASTER SUPPER

April 1943 is inscribed in our people's memory as the time of the Warsaw Ghetto Uprising. This was a fight waged by people, mostly young, who were strong and brave and fought without hope of winning. In desperation, they fought for their dignity, and they astonished the world with their bravery.

I watched the smoke and flames of the ghetto from a distance, through a tall window in the dining room of my employers. It was the time of the Easter holiday, celebrated in that household by eating traditional, good, homemade food and by drinking alcoholic beverages. The most free and willing to help himself that evening was Mr. Hoffman, the paternal grandfather of little Janush, whose parents had been taken to the concentration camps about a year ago by the Gestapo. Having had some drink, the older man became frivolous and talkative. He gave a broad view of the political situation and made predictions for the future. At that point I could relax. But I suddenly became alert when he said, "As for the burning ghetto, we have to admit that the Germans really do a good job for us. We had to get rid of the Jews in our country. And there are so many — about 3 million — of them. We would not be able to do it alone. So let them — the Jews — die there, jump from the high window thinking they will escape fire; let them run away to be soon entrapped. Let them throw their children away from the choking smoke. Let them scream for help. I do not care. They will come out of their hiding places. They should be treated like rats."

All this was said by a man who was well-off economically and socially. He talked so easily about political situations, and half drunk, he humorously praised the good food, prepared and served in a very traditional way, our beautiful Christian way. And you could say that it had been made with love, he said as much with a bow toward the hostess. She smiled and kept quiet. She knew the work was done, as usual, by me, at a time when I was deeply disturbed and worried about my child. Earlier today, on his third birthday, he had developed high fever and a swollen neck. The same morning he was operated on in a children's hospital and brought home still sedated. He slept while I prepared, served, and tried to eat this Easter meal. I was deeply worried, constantly listening to see if he had woken up yet. Meanwhile, our guest was quite relaxed, entertaining himself and the other guests around the table. He felt good, almost happy.

VACATION

The hot summer of 1944 arrived. My son's health was not good. He was coughing, anemic, looking pale and apathetic. He badly needed a vacation out of the city. I thought of one of the little towns located just outside the city and spread between the railroad line and the Vistula River. There, the small houses were surrounded by wonderfully fragrant pine trees; no smoke, no bad smells, just nice fresh air. My employer, the lady of the house where I had been working for about two years already, gave me permission to take a leave. I asked around and found a home in the country just where I wanted and where a maid was needed. Again, I got work not for pay, just for a place to sleep for me and Jerzy and food for me. I would share my portion with him. I agreed to these terms but demanded permission to take one hour every afternoon to be alone with my child. They agreed.

There were three people in the house: an old man, his wife, and a daughter. These two women would commute daily to the city. They worked and had their social life kept from me and the man. It seemed to me that they were involved in some underground political activities. This I found out only a few weeks later when they warned me about the upcoming uprising against the Germans and advised me to take the train back to Warsaw because I may have found myself cut off and would have to remain in that house with just the man.

This warning showed not only that they cared about me and Jerzy but, first, that they were well informed about the political events. This knowledge was limited to just a few activists. Second, it showed that they gave the man, the husband and father, little respect and trust. The man was an angry, frustrated one and extremely stingy. There was no food stored in the house. He did the daily food shopping for the family. Bread in the house was under his control. He would give me my daily portion and provide nothing for the child. He gave a whole loaf to the dog. It was a big, angry, and dangerous animal that tolerated only the old man. His love for the dog was also expressed by feeding him chunks of some kind of meat and bones. He never trusted me or let me cut off pieces of the meat to cook for dinner. I was envious; I would have also liked some meat. Once, he bought three pork chops. I prepared them and served them to the family. I was not eating in the dining room. After the dinner, the man came to the kitchen, asking, "Weren't the cutlets delicious?" I replied, "I do not know. I served all three to the table." "Right, it is okay. They were so expensive," he said.

He showed his anger whenever I took my hour off every day. Shortly, it became my way of asserting my dignity. My personal relations with the man was really not so important since Jerzy soon made some friends in the area and played with them all day outside. He looked better and his health had visibly improved. But I felt that something unusual was happening around us, that something in the air was changing.

One day, we found out that the German soldiers were all gone. In fact, they had left in the night leaving only a few behind to keep order and discipline at a war-prisoner's camp for the Russians that existed in the woods nearby. Usually, the camp was guarded by many armed Germans, but now it presented a changed situation. The Russians, disoriented, called to us, the people on the other side of barbed-wire fence. They asked for food and information. In this new situation, and with my kind ladies away, the old man became wild and more threatening. He said that he knew that I was "Asiatic." I did not know what it meant, but it did not sound good based on his tone. Furthermore, there was no food left in the house, and he said that he did not intend to get any more.

I remembered the women's earlier warning and decided to leave. But the trains were not going anymore and I found myself in a trap. With my child and a small bag I set out by foot, hoping to find some solution. It came in the form of a horse-driven wagon which made room for the two of us. On the way back to Warsaw, I learned that the Germans were leaving the city and an uprising would start very soon. In fact, it started the next day with the aim to chase and beat the fleeing Germans and to meet the Russians who were approaching Warsaw to liberate the capital. This plan did not work as expected. The Germans managed to kill 300,000 people in Warsaw, forcing the remaining population to leave the city. And after bombing it, they burned down the town systematically. They left only ruins.

During the duration of the Polish Uprising, I and my child suffered together with the Polish people. We had to hide in cellars which served as our shelters. We experienced the lack of food and the other hardships. But the liberation felt close. In the meantime, I got an offer to join a little hospital where the wounded Polish soldiers were getting help. The people around us continued to evacuate the city. They feverishly packed their possessions; the lucky ones had carts, or anything on wheels, while the others had to leave on foot, taking only what they could carry. They left their homes to the fierce enemy. I and my baby made the trip later, when we were evacuated from the hospital where I had worked for over twelve weeks.

No More Light

LOOTING

The hospital for fighters wounded in the 1944 Warsaw uprising was located close to the home in which we lived with my employers. The hospital was set up in a large apartment owned by a rich woman, a countess. When the evacuation order came, she, like everybody else, had to leave the city. The difference was that Germans were courteous to her and let her use their car, while others had to walk. They also promised to help her come back and retrieve some possessions, but they never did and she waited in vain.

In particular, the countess was extremely worried about a big tapestry hanging on a wall of the makeshift hospital. She let us know that the piece was very valuable and that any museum would pay a high price for it. Even, she said, if it had to be cut into pieces, she just wanted it taken out of town. I never saw anybody touch the tapestry. It remained there when we were forced to evacuate ourselves. But the countess's precious paintings were taken care of. Two young men took them out of the frames, rolled up the canvases, and disappeared.

The person brought by the Red Cross to manage the hospital gave us all Red Cross armbands, which we proudly wore. She watched the food and medical supplies. The pantry room was well-stocked. It felt like being in a fairy tale, standing there surrounded by flour, sugar, butter, and preserves of all kinds. This was food we hadn't seen for years. Now, it was carefully used to feed the group (the patients and the staff). In comparison, nobody cared about all other "valuables" in the house.

Initially, there was a feeling of respect for the countess's belongings. But this soon disappeared, and that is when the looting started. Quietly, people would enter the rooms where the armoires and drawers had been left open and good items had been left lying on the floor, rejected by previous scavengers. People looked for and took single items, things they said they suddenly realized they needed. This one took a warm blanket, this one a small valise, this one a coat or a warm sweater for the coming winter. One could not take more than one would be able to carry with them wherever they would be sent to.

Then I had my experience that involved jewelry. In one of the rooms, pieces of jewelry were found scattered on the floor. They were not too valuable looking, and seemed to have been rummaged through by those looters who, in a hurry, had selected valuable pieces worth taking. One could imagine them deliberating: "What about this pin with a pearl in the center? Is it a real pearl? Real or not, let me take it. And what about this bracelet? It does not look like real gold. But here is an inscription in French, and the date is 1812. Here is a second one-one inscribed to Grandma, the other to Grandpa. You take one, and I will take the other."

Then comes a moment of reflection: "What do I need jewelry for, especially from this strange place? Oh yes, I do need it because the war is still not over. I have no home and no security. My future is uncertain. I have no money and no valuables to start a new life in whatever new place I am evacuated to."

This was one part of the reasoning to justify looting, the other was the certainty that the Germans were only waiting for us to leave the countess's apartment, now the hospital, before they would start looting themselves. It was no secret that they were doing this already in surrounding houses. This work they assigned to the Ukrainian divisions. They were ordered to break into apartments, which hadn't been closed up well by the evacuated owners. They were to select and bring down to the street the best items, hoard them, and watch until the trucks came to collect them and take them away to facilities where they were sorted and sent to Germany. This specific information I got from a Ukrainian soldier who watched the heap in front of the house in which I used to work and which was now empty. The soldier saw me with my son. He gave me a sign to take the small sheepskin coat from the top of the heap. The coat was a little too long for my three-year-old son, but he would grow into it in years to come. For a few years it was worn by my son and then later by other younger children. This example shows how we can find excuses for participating in looting. How, in times of great need or in a situation of social crisis, people behave as they might not otherwise.

In the hospital, people soon became better acquainted, looking for closeness and even friendship. My boy was nice and friendly. He was the only child in the group, and people were glad to be in our company. Among them was a middle-aged woman named Barbara. She was a well-educated person, spoke Polish, Russian and German fluently, and Polish acceptably well. She had some knowledge in medicine. She also wished to be with and help people. She had had two unfortunate marriages in the past, and, feeling lonely, took my boy and me under her wing. She announced that we would go to Cracow, but we would not stay in Cracow. Instead, we would all go to a nearby small town, Wieliczka, where she had friends. We would rent a room together. Suddenly, it was "we" and "together," which gave me a good feeling of warmth and security. Twelve days later we were still in Warsaw, living in this hospital in an empty city, among houses ruined by bombs. We have witnessed a city systematically being burned down. Finally, our trucks with the Red Cross signs arrived and took us to an open place near the railroad station. Our destination was now via Cracow to Wieliczka — as Barbara had decided — but we would have to wait three days for the train to take us there. For me Barbara became a fresh source of security.

The Red Tower

BARBARA

Our association with Barbara, the woman we met and became friendly with while we were staying at the hospital, became troublesome. She wanted to be close and friendly with my child but her needs, demands, and behavior came to seem improper if only because they were brought out in the presence of my child, who was always around us. She became even dangerous to us.

Barbara's financial needs grew rapidly once her parents arrived from evacuated Warsaw to Wieliczka and, since they were people of higher class and status, their needs were different from ours. She would say, "They eat sausage with fork and knife in hand, biting small pieces of bread, while simple people eat bread, biting small pieces of sausage. My father needs good alcoholic drinks; my mother needs daily doses of morphine." So Barbara needed money, and I was supposed to provide it. "Otherwise," she said, "I know you are Jewish. I would not go to Gestapo and betray you but what I know, I know."

She wanted money, but I refused to give the little I had to her, especially since I knew the demands were growing and that my weakness would give her a better position and power. It was getting dangerous. Barbara missed the company of handsome men, the good talking and adoration. She needed drinks but it had to be in good company. She wanted to get pregnant and have her own child, even if the father was a German, but was too patriotic to be with a German, she said, debating with herself. Soon after, Barbara was suffering from a toothache and went to a dental clinic for German officers. She did not return before the curfew. After midnight, she rang the bell downstairs and, half-drunk, came up accompanied by a young officer. I left the double bed we had been sharing and shared a small couch with my son, who was by now well awake and bewildered. He kept asking, "Who is the man? Why is he here?" It was not easy to calm him down. In the morning, the man was gone, but several times he paid us visits, forcing me to live with the danger of having a German officer in my home. Finally, the wondering and angry owner of the house gave me permission to move to a tiny storage room on the same floor.

Barbara continued to wear the Red Cross band, especially when going to the dental clinic. Her romance did not last long. She was really sad when the Germans left, taking away her friend/lover and who-knows-what in the future. At the same time, the Russians came, and a Russian officer was stationed in our home. It was not long before he came to me saying, "What a strange woman this Madame Barbara is. She speaks German. Her Russian is so good. She is educated and behaves so strange." The soldier was bewildered and I didn't want to discuss Barbara anymore. I distanced myself in spite of her attempts to keep a relationship with me and especially my son. A natural solution came when my husband appeared as a survivor after the war and took us away to Warsaw.

The Blind Soul

WAITING FOR THE TRAIN-ANTOSH

With excitement we transferred the hospital, loading all its supplies on the trucks marked Red Cross which were going to the train to Cracow. There a big hospital was supposed to take in the sick and wounded and us, the staff. For us three Barbara had other plans. Although we did not intend to remain in service with the Red Cross, we would not take off the Red Cross armband too soon. It gave us prestige in the eyes of people around us.

Our trip to the station was long and depressing. It led through empty streets, where only abandoned dogs and cats could be spotted. Houses were ruined by bombs or fire. Trucks driven by Germans or Ukrainian soldiers rushed by, loaded with plunder. The station, just a barn standing near the railroad tracks, was far away from the city. At this place we had to unload and wait for the train. The wait lasted three days. The days were sunny and warm. But the nights were cold, and my woolen blanket, taken from the countess's apartment, served us well. We badly needed food, water, and a fire to warm us outside this barn in a field. We really needed help, and it came from a small local clinic. They had taken in our hospitals' disabled and helpless. We had to provide for ourselves. But when we found the three of us in this difficult situation a young, strong man suddenly appeared near us. He was interested in my son and began talking to him. He was friendly to all of us and helped us with all the hard work. His name was Antosh, a nickname for Anthony. He was short, with dark hair and eyes and a pug nose. His looks, his way of moving, and the language he used showed that he was a peasant from the countryside.

Soon Antosh became a member of our family — and a very useful one. He wanted to travel with us in the hopes that, together, we would all survive and get back to our lives. He was trying to return to his wife and two children — a family he was cut off from by the war. In particular, he showed that he wanted to be alone with me. At one moment, when Barbara was away, he said, "I know that you are Jewish. You and your son are Jewish. And so am I. Let us keep close." Frightened, I said, "Mr. Antosh, do us all a great favor and disappear. Together we will increase the danger of being discovered." He granted my request. He did move away, but he remained in contact. We parted in Cracow, and Barbara, Jerzy, and I went to a nearby town where she had friends. Antosh knew our address and came several times to pay us short visits. The last time he came was after we had been liberated, freed from the Germans with the Russian soldiers around. He announced that he was going to Warsaw to look for anyone from his family or for a trace of them. He took the names of my family members and promised to search and leave word in the office of the Committee of Polish Jews located in Warsaw.

Intensive work was being done there to register the survivors and helping them in the search for family members. Two weeks after leaving, Antosh returned and told me that he did not find any of his people but that he had found out that my husband, the father of my child, was alive. He left me a small letter with the big news. Good, friendly Antosh left before my husband arrived.

Blue and White

END OF WAR

It was winter, 1945. Heavy artillery shooting could be heard in our small town of Wieliczka located near Cracow where my son and I lived. Now, the German soldiers we seldom saw looked frightened. Their courage and bravery seemed to be gone. One night, increasing fighting was heard on the streets of the town and we sensed the promise of freedom. We hid in a cellar until the morning came. The noise stopped; fights were over. Dead bodies, German and Russian, lay in the empty streets. It was a terrible sight for me and my boy. But all that meant that the war was ending. The Russians were already in town. Our liberators were quite busy, looking for spoils. What they wanted most was vodka and wrist watches. Vodka was used not only to drink but to exchange for other goods. Watches were their passion. They would wear them down the whole length of their arms.

A watch was always a good item for barter. It served well to get the favors of a girl or would be appreciated by one's family back home. We were first delighted by the presence of the Red Army, proud of our liberators. But then, seeing their unscrupulous looting, we were astonished. "Is this the famous Red Army?" we asked each other. With this same question I turned to the commandant of the town. In response to my question, he asked, "What happened? Did they rape you?" "No, they did not do this to me. But people in town wonder what kind of army the Red Army is." He explained, "Our good divisions we send to the serious battles still going on. The way to Berlin is still long. Here on the 'first line' in the streets, in the face-to-face fights, we use ex-prisoners. They are getting a chance to win their freedom — if they survived. Raping or plundering is forbidden, but if there were some looting we would not care much." The young commandant offered an apple to my son and gallantly let us out of his office.

On the way back home we saw some people on the highway busily crowded around dead horses. The animals had been killed in the night battles. Now frozen, belonging to nobody, they presented an easy and much-wanted source of meat for people. We rushed home, got sharp knives, and managed to cut a few nice pieces of meat. Some of it was ground and used for hamburgers or meatloaf. I made these meals to take on our daily trips to Cracow in search of other survivors.

In the city, some ground-floor apartments or other empty spaces were opened for survivors arriving from nearby Auschwitz. They were all still in the concentration camp's striped uniforms. Emaciated and weak, they were sitting on the streets in hopes of seeing and being seen by the people arriving in search of a familiar face. They would get up and form a line in front of a person who brought food. My meat smelled and tasted good, and the people were glad to have it. We would exchange a word or two, giving me an opportunity to look at them in a natural, human way.

The last of these daily trips to the city ended with my visit to the local office of the Committee of the Polish Jews, where I registered myself as a widow of Marek Bitter, assuming he had perished with his family.

Deserted

REUNION

In 1944, when only the eastern part of Poland had been liberated, the Polish government created a committee for Polish Jews. Their task was to give immediate help to people who survived the Holocaust. Both the government and the committee were functioning in Lublin, a town southeast of Warsaw. After the liberation of the western Warsaw, the whole capital was free of Germans and all the government's institutions moved back into the city. My husband, as vice-president of the committee, was responsible for social problems. That was all the committee at that time did. He was building new divisions of the organization in smaller towns. He had to provide the new divisions with the means (money, food, clothes, etc.) to help the needy. He was busy in Lublin and Warsaw, and he became very well known in the Jewish community. He was himself a survivor of two concentration camps. He was a very active person by nature and was able to fill the role of a much-needed leader quite well.

One day, when he arrived at the Warsaw office, which was always crowded and noisy, his co-worker and friend stopped him and said, "Sit down and listen. We have some news for you." "More news. Don't we have enough news?" he replied. "Just sit and listen. Your wife and your son survived. They are in a town near Cracow. Here is the address." The trains were not running yet — there were just locomotives with wagons running on quickly-assembled temporary tracks. To travel, one had to jump on a wagon. Another solution was to find a place on one of the military trucks running on the roads. One such truck, a jeep, arrived one day at the little house where we lived. The driver, a soldier, came to my room and asked me follow him outside. I went.

"Someone is waiting for you," he said. "Oh, you want to say that my husband came? Is he alive?" I was shivering, and said, "What if this is a mistake? People seek in hope and are disappointed." I could see nobody at first, but then he came into view, my husband Marek, emerging from the back of the vehicle. We looked at each other in amazement.

He asked about his son, and soon two little boys arrived from the playground, one in a too-long sheepskin coat. He started talking to us, not paying much attention to his father. He called him "Mister." I corrected him, saying, "This is your father." He said, "Mister Father." How strange the word "father" sounded to me coming from my son. And what did his father feel hearing it? The boy was one year old when he and I left the family. Now, in 1945, he was four years old, a stranger to his father. There were no embraces or much kissing. Rather, there was embarrassed silence. That afternoon guests came to greet the survivor, my husband. When they finally left us alone, I questioned him. "What about Mama? And your sisters? And their husbands?" "All perished" was the answer. "When, where, how? Nobody survived?" "Nobody. Just the three of us." He was a good storyteller, and as he told me of his life those past years, he talked and hardly asked me any questions. He said that he knew that I would survive and save our son. He was almost sure of that, and that belief had forced him to find a way to survive.

The day ended, and like any old married couple, we went to bed. I did not want to be "taken" as any woman. Physical closeness could not break the heavy feeling of estrangement created by the years of separation and by the events and experiences we had each had. He was a stranger to me. I needed to be alone, to get acquainted, to be courted by him. I had to start loving and desiring this man all over again. I don't know what he felt; we never spoke about that. The wall between us remained forever.

I think that a similar situation existed between him and our son. The past years with all of their horrible experiences had done so much damage to our feelings and sensitivity. This loving and friendly and joyful man told me that he could not get close to his own son. He knew he was hurting him, but he could not help it. My son still complains of his father's strange behavior. But he could not recover those years of being with a child he had lost because of the war.

As for me, I still could not fulfill his dream of having a wife like his mother, one who took great care of all his needs, who kept the household in perfect condition by getting up first in the morning and going to sleep last in the evening. This was not my vision of life. Instead, I declared that I wanted to work; I wished to have a career of my own. I wanted to study, get an education, and attain a high position. All this I could easily achieve.

But he was older than me and set in his ideas. His war experiences had solidified them. He had to be great right now, to be loved and respected as he was. And he was. As much as he was disappointed with my performance as a wife, he took great pride in my achievements. His horrible experiences during the Holocaust left him with a damaged heart and caused his death at a still early age of 53 in the year 1965.

Children

RETURN TO WARSAW

The next day after Marek Bitter, my husband, found us in Wieliczka, the town near Cracow where I was living with our son during the last month of the war, we took a quick leave and rushed to the capital. Work demanded his presence there.

Warsaw is divided by the Vistula River. On the west side of the river the city lay in ruins; few people could find a place to live there or function amid such terrible destruction. Most life centered on the east side of the city, called Praga. The apartments there were crowded by old tenants and by newcomers coming from the camps or various hiding places, forests, including the many repatriates returning from Russia. The newly created government institutions and the office of the Committee for Polish Jews were also located in Praga. Thanks to relief help, mainly from American Jewish organizations, the committee was busy providing the needy with food, supplies, clothes and money. The committee was, for many, the place to go to search for the lost, meet survivors and exchange information.

We were assigned to a two-bedroom apartment to share with another family. The apartment was just a few houses away from the offices of the committee. That proximity caused not only my husband but all three of us to become involved in committee life.

At that time very few children were around. It was harder still to find a full family with a young child. We were an anomaly. People wanted closeness; they wanted to share our company, our modest meals, and mostly our child. After meeting him once, they treated him as an old friend, calling him by name, grabbing or petting him affectionately. As a result, Jerzy always a quiet boy, became nervous and unhappy. To change the situation we placed him in a place called Children's Home, located in a beautiful, healthy suburban village. The home took some Jewish children, mostly those coming out from hiding places like monasteries or those returned to the Jewish community by the Christian families who had hidden them. The manager of the house was another survivor, a famous pedagogue, Luba Bielicke. She was an excellent teacher, but even she did not understand the trouble my son was experiencing. As often happens, the children in the home tormented each other just for fun. In my son's case, they confused my son Yurek by calling him a Jew, the meaning of which he did not understand. They also informed him that his name was really Bitter. This name he did not know and had not accepted yet. He still thought that his and my name was Medzinski, like during the war. We had not informed him of the truth yet because he was too confused by all the other changes going on in his life. He asked to be taken back home and shortly afterward started attending kindergarten as Bitter and as a Jew — whatever that identity meant to this four-and-a-half year old child.

Some bigger problems resulting from the Holocaust and the war arose in our house. Too many people were coming and bringing their memories. They had an urgent need to share them with friends. Excited and loud talks took place in three languages - Polish, Yiddish, and Russian. The child was always around. He was anxious when he did not understand the language spoken and asked, "Speak Polish, please." Even worse was that the subject was often inappropriate for a child. When the people came back from Russia they demanded our immediate attention. They wanted us to hear what horrors they had gone through. But when the survivors of the concentration camps started to tell of their horrors the Russians had to give up, listen, and wait until the time for their stories came. As I said, there was no way to protect this attentive child from listening to the stories told and retold. He asked questions and asked for more stories. The survivors needed to talk, to have the children listen to their stories. In the case of my son, I am convinced that the sadness now felt by some viewers of his pictures has its source in those stories of the Holocaust. His work also reflects his own feelings of pain and diminished joy of life as well as his compassion for the suffering of those around him. Frightful dreams, still occurring to this now-sixty-year-old man, have — I am sure — their roots in the events of that Holocaust time.

Stories of the Holocaust reach us in different forms, like books and films. Their purpose is to keep the record of this suffering in our hearts and memory. Although this suffering cannot be understood — there is no answer to the question of *Why* — it cannot be forgotten, especially by the *Children.* "Mama, what does it mean, Kampf?" This was the first question our boy asked, because the word had been spoken so often and with such passion. And how do you explain to a child that we have to fight fascism, dictatorship, terror, poverty and all forms of hatred shown by people to people? All they want is to live in peace and friendship.

Shelter

THE BLESSED FAMILY

A full Jewish family with a four or five-year-old boy could hardly be found after liberation. Ours was an extremely lucky case, and our outward appearance indicated to others that we were a united and happy family. But it soon became clear that there was none of that happiness and harmony so desperately needed by the child. Instead, there was a fierce relationship between the parents.

Marek and I survived thanks to our own personalities. Together the personalities did not work; they led to friction. Our needs were different, as were our ways of expressing and fulfilling them. He had a strong voice. When he spoke up, it sounded like shouting to me and the child. I had to shout to ask him not to shout. "That is the way I speak," he would say. And the boy was crying. I didn't like the loudness. We also fought about our way of life. He wanted the house full of people but the child and I needed privacy and intimacy. He wanted his domineering role, but I needed my independence. He dreamed about a submissive wife and a house like his parents had. I could not even think of that. He really loved the two of us but never learned to listen and consider our feelings. My and our boy's achievements were the subject of his bragging to others, but he could not learn to praise us directly. Marek was charming, good looking, and easily drew attention and won friends. He was witty, could sing well, was able to tell good stories, and could lead good conversations especially on politics. He needed an audience when he was in good health and even when he became sick this was his first remedy. You felt that he was the only real SURVIVOR. We just happened to survive. He was as good a husband and father as he could be. He was a good provider for the family. But when I would earn extra income for my work I thought it better not to tell him of any amount higher than his own salary. The idea of a divorce did appear and was discussed, but our conversation was overheard by the child. "There will be no divorce because a child needs a Mama and a Tata," the child said sadly. In the end we did not divorce. We continued to live together. Marek would joke: "At least we have a great, interesting life. You are never bored with me." That was true.

Now, what our son remembers most was the time when I was away for several weeks and he and his father were home alone. At that time, he, my husband, was different. He gave his son previously unknown love and attention, though he admitted that he often felt alone, not needed in this trio consisting of me, the boy who grew up with me, and him, the father who missed the first four years in his son's life. But the responsibility for all this loss and pain lies with those hostile forces who pushed our lives in the wrong directions.

Locked

NEW LIFE

In a small, overcrowded apartment in Warsaw two families started a new postwar life. The three of us — the Bitters — were local survivors. We shared the apartment with a middle-aged couple who spent the war in Russia and had all returned to Poland. Marek Bitter, already engaged in his work with the Committee for Polish Jews, had to face numerous, urgent, and difficult social problems daily. He felt strong, needed, and in demand in political circles. The house was full of guests; he was always entertaining, joking, singing, serving homemade food — Jewish dishes. He was sent to America to speak in Madison Square Garden and various other places about the events during the war and about great needs existing; about the survivors and their expectations from the "American brothers and sisters." Then he made a short visit to speak in France and Switzerland and triumphantly returned home.

"I certainly would not sacrifice my work for you," he would say. I just do not remember why and on what occasions he said it. He also declared, "I do not know how to handle children. You take care of him." Four years of separation did so much harm to the relationship between him and his son. Physically, he seemed to be in good condition in spite of his terrible experiences in Majdanek and other concentration camps and the rough conditions in the woods where he lived with the partisans. But shortly a serious heart condition was discovered, making our family's life even harder.

The other family sharing the apartment was named Zelicki. Mrs. Zelicki was a little over 40. Still as young as her husband, she preferred to stay home, socialize, read books, etc. She did not want to go out and work. She did not want a child. She had aborted pregnancies at the time when she and her husband were afraid of being arrested as communists. This was before the war. And during the war she remembered her marches through the snow to bring food to him, in prison. It was never made clear why he, an old communist, was arrested in Soviet Russia. But he seemed to have forgotten the past. He loved children and wanted them in his family. He was full of energy, already working and was wanted in many important posts because of his abilities. While working with the Committee of Polish Jews, Mr. Zelicki built numerous cooperative workshops where the survivors were employed.

But at home he was visibly unfulfilled, and he soon found the answer to his needs. After celebrating New Year's Day in 1946, he left home and never returned. He spent the rest of his life with another woman who was younger, loving and devoted. Soon they had a son. Thirty years later that son was the Israeli ambassador to the United States. They also had a daughter. She settled in Australia, where she worked as a chemist. Her mother later came to live there with her after Mr. Zelicki's death in Israel.

As for the old Mrs. Zelicki, she punished her ex-husband for leaving her in two ways. First, she refused to take any help, financial or otherwise, from him, even when she was in need. Secondly, she declared that she would never grant him a divorce. The punishment, although unpleasant for the new family Zelicki, did not change their social or economic status much. Due to his talent, Mr. Zelicki was appointed a vice-minister in the Polish government. The family gracefully used the privileges deriving from his high position. One of which was the ability to obtain, in secret, documents to legally leave the country and go abroad. This happened in the late '60's, when a wave of anti-Semitism forced many Jews to leave their jobs, homes, and cultural roots to emigrate. They went to Israel. The family worked hard, was surrounded by many friends, and was highly respected. The old Mrs. Zelicki also went to Israel eventually. She spent the rest of her life in loneliness in Jerusalem. She never forgave the betrayal.

My Sweet, Sweet Mother

IN SEARCH OF THEIR OWN CHILD: THE TAILOR'S TALE

Shortly after the war ended we badly needed the services of a tailor. There was plenty of cloth sent from America, but this cloth had to be treated by a professional. We soon found a tailor. He and his wife lived near us, and, shortly, we learned about their tragedy. During the dangerous days of deportation to death camps they were hiding with their infant son in a village. For some money a peasant had let them live in his house from the beginning of the war. There the child was born. But soon, with the growing terror, the owner of the house got frightened, and the tailor's family no longer felt welcome there or secure. They decided to seek a new place to live. For some reason, possibly because they spoke German fluently, they chose to go and hide in Germany. But that plan would not work if they took the baby. At the threshold of a nice house they left their baby with a letter saying that the child had already been baptized and begging the owners to take him in and save him.

Their plan to save their own lives worked. After the war, they rushed to the place where they expected to find their son. The people in the house remembered the case of the child found by the previous residents, who had transferred him to the orphans' home and left. After a short trip, they found the orphanage burned to the ground and nobody to ask about the children of the house. The desperate mother turned to a Russian officer stationed with a group of soldiers in a little hospital near us. She needed a means of transportation and the authority of a military man to search around. First she was told that in the bombing of the house all had been killed, her son included. Then she found a nun who had worked in the home and who told her that the child had been taken away by a couple of *Volksdeutschen* who had adopted him. Later the couple had to flee and had most probably gone to Germany because of the angry feelings of Poles toward collaborators.

In desperation the mother continued the search. She got information that the man had really fled to Germany but that his wife and the child they had adopted were in some small distant town. Upon going to this town, the woman found an unmistakable picture of her son enlarged in the window of a local photographer. After being given the woman's address, the mother found the proper house and let herself in. She saw her child and presented her claim to the woman, who immediately became furious and threw her out of the house, claiming that this was *her* child, that she had given birth to him. The tailor's wife, with the help of a Russian officer, turned to local court. The judges gathered that same day, and based on physical similarities between the Jewish mother and the boy, they soon decided: "The Jewess is the real mother, and she can take the boy home, where the father will be, though they are both strangers to the boy."

The next day the potentially happy parents realized that they had brought home a most unhappy boy. He was angry because he had been taken away from his beloved mother, from his nice house with a garden and maybe a well-loved dog, to a small, one-room apartment with a long table piled with tailor's items. The boy declared that he hated the place and the people. He said that he had his parents there; he hated the ones here. He called them Jews as an insult. He knew how to hurt.

Even now, I can't stop thinking about the part-German woman "there," all alone without her husband, who left her for political reasons and without the boy they had adopted when he was "available," abandoned by his real parents in the storm of war. She loved the boy and had hoped to have a good son. Would he have been good to anybody after such an experience? Did they all ever find happiness?

Wave of Silence

A STORY FROM FRANCE

Something similar to what happened to the tailor's family in Poland happened to a family of our friends in France. A Jewish couple had left Poland and come to live in Paris with their baby boy. They were respected and well-liked by a circle of friends, both Jewish and Gentile. When bad times came, many Jews were arrested and disappeared. Our friends entrusted their beloved child to a family of their closest Gentile friends living outside Paris in nice, healthy surroundings. What started as a vacation became — with growing terror — a situation as good as anybody could wish for the child. The unavoidable fate happened to his parents. Only hopeless news kept coming. There was no reason to believe that this couple would survive while millions were killed.

At this time, a Gentile couple from Switzerland appeared. Through comrades from the Communist Party, they met the Gentile family keeping the little boy and learned the whole story. Childless and very wealthy, they were ready to adopt the boy but with one condition: their whereabouts would never be given to anybody. Being convinced that the boy's parents had perished, the people thought that the offer was possibly the best option for the boy. After numerous consultations with others they agreed to the offer and the condition.

The boy continued to grow up, happy and immensely loved. This lasted until the end of the war. The tragedy occurred when the biological parents, who had somehow miraculously survived, returned to Paris and demanded the child. Facing a wall of silence, the mother pleaded and asked permission to just see the child from a distance. She swore never to go closer. The friends broke their promise never to give out the address. The mother went to Switzerland and, seeing her son, could not control herself and went inside the house. Without saying a word, she was recognized by the man of the house. "You are the mother of the child whom we love so much. He is yours. You take him whenever you find it proper."

But as with the tailor's child, the boy had all the feelings for his Swiss parents and none for his biological ones. He behaved obediently, never said an improper word, always controlled his feelings. As a result he later had to get psychiatric help. All five people suffered; there was no good solution for them.

As soon as he reached the proper age, the boy left for Israel and joined a kibbutz. While polite but cold to his Paris parents, he was always warm and caring toward the Swiss ones, especially to the woman when her husband died. He inherited their fortune, which was given to the kibbutz. I heard the story at the time I came to Israel, and I could feel the immense suffering of all involved.

Tale

ELISABETH

The following happened in my own family. Several years after the war we wanted to adopt a child, "a girl with a pink ribbon in her hair," as my husband used to say. We took her from a children's home located in a nice woody suburb of Warsaw called Otvock. As we were told by the director of the home, Elisabeth came from a fine family. Her loving and educated parents had cherished great hopes for their smart little girl. When faced with the deadly dangers of wartime, they must have been glad to find a Polish Gentile family, not far away, near the Baltic Sea, who agreed to take in the child. Years of war passed; the parents did not return; nobody claimed the child. The Polish father made the decision to return her to the Jewish community. He brought her to this good "home for children" so nicely located and with children her own age and a supervising staff. He even received some money as compensation for their expenses, etc.

As good as the home was, the authorities maintained that adoption was a better solution for an orphan. So Elisabeth arrived to live with us. She became a good companion to our son and the little girl of my husband's dreams, with or without ribbons in her hair. She was bright, strong-willed, and demanding. She wanted to establish clearly her rights in the family. This came in time when we thought we could speak to her about adoption. When we asked her, "Would you like to call us Mama and Tata as Yurek, our son, does?" She said, "But I have already a Mama and a Tata, at the seaside where I came from." We were shocked and did not even know how to react.

Shortly after that incident some others occurred. The tata came to claim his child from the Jewish committee. He asked, "Where is Elisabeth? She had to live in the home," he said. He wanted her to come to their house for vacation. Under pressure, Elisabeth returned to the home, then was taken back to her mama and tata at the seaside.

Shortly, letters began arriving from the child asking us to take her out of there. "Tata drinks. There are scandals at home. I want to be with Yurek — in your home." After all the events in the past and insecure about the future, we were not able to take her back. With the assistance of a social worker, she was returned to the children's home and later adopted by highly educated people who loved her dearly and gave all they could. We were asked not to show too much attention or any affection to her. She needed to establish clearly her place in a new family.

Escape

Printed in the United States
By Bookmasters